UNCOMMON WOMEN

pirates

Sarah K. Davis

Uncommon Women: Pirates

Scobre Educational
42982 Osgood Road
Fremont, CA 94539

www.scobre.com
info@scobre.com

Scobre Educational publications may be purchased for educational, business, or sales promotional use.

Cover design by Sara Radka
Layout Design by Nikki Ramsay
Edited by Kirsten Rue and Lauren Dupuis-Perez
Copyedited by Malia Green
Images sourced from iStock, Shutterstock, Newscom, and Alamy

ISBN: 978-1-62920-585-4 (hardcover)
ISBN: 978-1-62920-584-7 (eBook)

table of contents

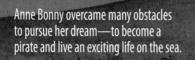

Anne Bonny overcame many obstacles to pursue her dream—to become a pirate and live an exciting life on the sea.

Chapter One
ANNE BONNY, PART I

Anne Bonny's life was controversial from the beginning. She was born in Ireland around 1700, with the name Anne Cormac. Her father William Cormac was married to Mrs. Cormac, who was not Anne's mother. William Cormac brought Anne into his home, introduced her to Mrs. Cormac, and told everyone that Anne was an orphaned girl he wanted to raise as his own. Due to the unusual circumstances, there was a rumor that Anne was actually William's daughter. The gossip reached Mrs. Cormac and once she discovered Anne was not an orphan, but instead William's child from another relationship, she realized she had been deceived. She became very angry and threatened to send Anne away.

William originally wanted nothing to do with Anne, but he loved the little girl and her mother, who had been a maid in the Cormac household. Instead of staying in Ireland, William moved Anne and her mother to Charles Town. In 1783, the city became known as Charleston, South Carolina. They lived on a small plantation on the Black River. At first, William worked as a lawyer, but he

> ## DID YOU KNOW?
> People from Ireland started immigrating to the U.S. in the 1600s. Reasons included expensive housing and mistreatment due to religious beliefs.

changed careers and invested in plantations when he found out how much money could be made. He became very wealthy, owned slaves, and was a man of high status in the community. The family lived happily together for several years after their arrival in South Carolina. Sadly, Anne's mother became sick with typhoid fever and died when Anne was only about 13 years old.

After the death of her mother, Anne and William spent more time together. Anne followed her father everywhere. She learned about her father's work, which included planting and harvesting procedures, as well as the running of the plantations. She acquired so much knowledge from her father that if he had to leave for a few days, Anne was left in charge of the plantations. Perhaps it was her closeness to her father, or how involved she was in

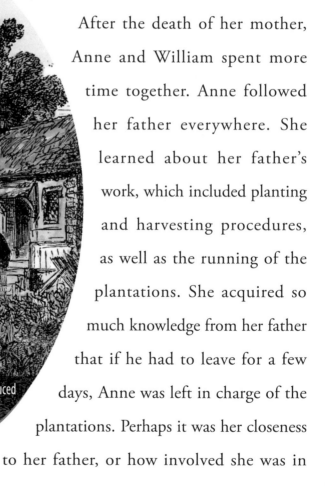

Plantations in the South in the 17th century produced a variety of crops. They often relied on slave labor and had harsh working conditions.

working, but Anne was not well-suited for the rich society of Charles Town and the other women in her social circle. As a teenager, she swore, ran wild, and it was rumored that she tried to stab a servant girl and attacked a potential suitor, leaving him bloody.

In one particular incident, she tried to ride Satan, a large black horse, who was too wild to be ridden. She ignored the warnings of one of the slaves, Romulus, who was in charge of the horses. William had banned Anne from riding this particular horse, and Romulus was not allowed to let her ride it. Romulus tried to stop her, but Anne mounted the horse anyway. Satan bucked as soon as he took a few steps, and his feet came down on Romulus, killing him. Anne's reaction was to go riding anyway. This type of decision-making was characteristic of Anne and her desire to do what she wanted—no matter the cost.

When William found out that Anne had disobeyed him, was responsible for Romulus's death, and had gone riding rather than get help, he could not believe that his daughter would be so heartless. He had also been hearing rumors about her spending time in taverns and drinking. Her reputation was starting to hurt his businesses. When he confronted her, Anne replied that she was going to meet her future husband and got into an argument with her father. At the time, Anne was engaged to a medical student, but she insisted on marrying James

Bonny, a poor sailor-turned-pirate. At that time, being the daughter of a wealthy plantation owner meant that Anne was supposed to marry someone from another rich family. William thought James was not worthy of his daughter and told Anne that if she married James, she would not **inherit** any money.

However, Anne had other plans. She did not want to spend the rest of her life in Charles Town as a high-society wife. She craved adventure. From a young age, Anne developed an obsession with pirates and the stories she read about them in newspapers and books. Piracy in the Americas was very common between 1650 and 1725, also known as the Golden Age of Piracy. Due to the Spanish exploration of the New World in the 1500s, ships would travel back across the ocean to Europe. Ships from other European countries arrived in the 1600s, and the treasures aboard those ships attracted pirates who wanted that wealth for themselves. Around the same time Anne was arguing with her father, something was causing fear among Charles Town's residents—the famous pirate named Blackbeard.

In 1718, Edward Teach, more commonly known as Blackbeard, caused fear among Charles Town's residents when he and his crew appeared. Blackbeard was a ruthless pirate who had control of a flotilla—a large number of ships—in the city's port. He and his crew had taken a group of residents of Charles Town hostage. When many of Blackbeard's men fell ill, he sent two of his crew with a

The Golden Age of Piracy was a dangerous time to be a sailor. Pirates often used trickery to lure ships closer so they could board, fight, and steal their valuables.

Blackbeard the pirate tried to take over Charles Town, the town in which Anne Bonny lived. He may have inspired her to seek the pirate lifestyle.

hostage to the port to get medicine, but they did not return. Blackbeard, thinking they had been taken as prisoners by the governor, threatened to burn every ship in the port and attack the entire city. Luckily, the governor and Blackbeard were able to come to an agreement and Charles Town was saved.

Anne ran away from home in 1718. She snuck out of her house with only a few belongings and rode Satan to meet up with James Bonny. While he was a good-looking man, James was not well-respected among his fellow pirates. Whether Anne was attracted to him because of her desire for adventure or for the appeal of life as a pirate is unknown. Regardless, they married and decided to sail to Nassau, in the Bahamas, known then as New Providence Island. The port of Nassau was an ideal spot for pirates because of its location and all the different types of boats in its harbors. It was also too shallow for large naval ships, and the hills around the harbor gave pirates a view of potential victims or rival vessels. In the early 1700s, around 1,500

pirates made their home there thanks to these favorable conditions.

However, Anne quickly grew bored with her new life in Nassau. She realized that James was a jealous and weak man. In Nassau, James learned that the government would reward people who reported information about pirates. James betrayed his fellow pirates for money. To be a traitor against fellow pirates was considered one of the worst crimes possible for a pirate. When Anne found out what James was doing, her hatred for him grew.

She soon became infatuated with a pirate captain named John Rackham, nicknamed Calico Jack due to his famous striped cotton pants. They fell in love, and Anne asked Calico Jack to take her away. She asked James for a divorce, since they were still married, but James refused. Calico Jack offered to pay James for Anne, a request that normally would have ended in a duel due to it being so offensive to the husband, but James was too much of a coward to stand up to Calico Jack. Instead, James told the governor. Since James worked for the governor by informing on pirates and helping to capture them, he thought the governor would help him keep his wife, and James was right. The governor

Calico Jack was a fierce leader who gave Anne Bonny the opportunity to become a pirate and join his crew.

threatened to have Anne publicly whipped if she didn't immediately return to James, which was the common punishment at this time for a woman leaving her husband for another man. As she had done with her father, Anne continued to follow her own wishes.

In the midst of the governor's threats, Jack and Anne started conspiring to steal a ship named the *Curlew*. This way, the two could get away from James, the governor, and Nassau. By flirting with two of the *Curlew's* sailors, Anne was able to obtain information about the ship, including when the night guard changed on the boat, and she and Jack came up with a clever plan. At night, they returned to the ship when most of its crew were at a saloon in town. They snuck onto the boat, and Anne, armed with a sword and pistol, helped tie up the two crewmen on board. The rest of Jack's pirate gang then joined them on the ship and they sailed safely toward the sea, but not before putting the prisoners on a small boat and sending them back to shore. They sailed away, and this journey marked the beginning of Anne's career as an infamous female pirate.

Battles in the ocean were commonplace; pictured here is the boat named the Brethren of the Coast attacking three Spanish galleons.

Chapter Two

ANNE BONNY, PART II

Anne's route to becoming a pirate was unusual for two reasons. The first reason was that most men became sailors before they became pirates, but Anne became a pirate first. In the 1600s and 1700s, it was common for boys to start working on ships when they were teenagers. They would work as the assistants of more experienced sailors and learn all about the basics of being on a ship. Life on a boat was often dangerous, and many sailors were killed or injured at sea. As a result, it was difficult for captains to keep good workers because many of the men quit. Also, during this time period, it was common for captains to send groups of men to the ports to round up new sailors by tricking them or kidnapping them. Anne avoided this more common route of becoming a pirate.

Many boys during the 17th century dreamed of working aboard a ship.

The second reason her path was unusual was because she had to dress like a man in order to be a convincing pirate. As a woman, it was unthinkable for Anne to want the life of a pirate. At this time in history, people thought that women were too fragile and weak to do the physical labor required of sailors. By dressing as a man, she could fight alongside the men and no one would suspect anthing. One of the first things she did was cut her hair. She wore only one or two sets of clothes, which were usually dirty and wet: a loose-fitting jacket with buttons made of bone or wood, knee length pants to allow for movement, a handkerchief tied on her head, a sash around her waist, leather shoes, and the pistol and machete (a large knife with a wide blade) she carried at all times.

During the next six months after taking over the *Curlew*, Anne fought alongside Calico Jack and the other members of the crew. They collected a small fortune in gold, silver, and other valuable items by robbing ships around the Bahamas. Sometimes there were violent battles. Anne's skills with weapons proved as good, if not better, than her fellow male pirates. She loved life beneath the Jolly Roger—the pirate flag with a black background and a white skull and bones—even if it meant dressing like a man. It is likely that she wore women's clothes in private, while on the ship around her own familiar crew. In order to be

Once pirates took control of a ship, it was often chaotic as the pirates searched for treasure and fought the crew.

taken seriously as a pirate, she would have had to dress like a man whenever Calico Jack and his pirates robbed other ships.

Life on a ship included a lot of free time to play cards and games, drink, and maintain the ship. Every day was different and the adventures were plenty. However, the appeal of being a pirate often wore off quickly due to a lack of medical help, rotten food, rats aboard the ship, and crowded conditions.

After a successful raid, pirate celebrations were often held at taverns on shore and turned into rowdy parties.

Plus, there were the risks of storms, disease, fights among the crew—or, on rare occasions when an offense was committed, a pirate could be thrown overboard or left alone on a deserted island. Calico Jack's new ship, the *Curlew*, was Anne's home for the first stage of her pirate career. Unfortunately, not everyone was as accepting of her as Calico Jack. Early in her time aboard the *Curlew*, another pirate challenged her and they dueled. He did not want a woman as a part of their crew. Anne won the duel and immediately proved her worth as a pirate.

Suddenly, however, Anne began to get sick in the mornings. She noticed she couldn't move as quickly and had trouble with her balance. She was pregnant. Since there wasn't a doctor on their ship, Calico Jack and Anne left behind their life of piracy and sailed to Cuba. The island of Cuba was a safe place for pirates and their families at the time. There are two versions of what happened next. The first story is that the baby girl that Anne gave birth to died soon after. The second story claims that Anne gave her baby to another family to raise. No matter which story is true, Calico Jack and Anne eventually returned to the Bahamas without a child and began planning their next act of piracy. They longed to be pirates again.

Pirates had a lot of free time on the ships. They could practice their fighting skills or catch up on some sleep.

Soon after their return to the *Curlew*, they spotted a large ship with two masts. The cannons were loaded and the sails were raised as they made plans to sail alongside the big ship and get aboard. The other crew members stood on the deck waving their swords. However, the captain of the other ship started waving a white flag, the symbol of surrender. Calico Jack and his pirates took over the Dutch ship and found chests of valuable silk and other items that could be sold for large amounts of money on shore. As they had done before, the pirates convinced some of the Dutch sailors to join the pirates in their search for treasure and adventure, and many of them did become pirates and join Calico Jack's crew.

One sailor in particular caught Anne's eye. While she had been faithful to Calico Jack, Anne started to spend time with this good-

A Dutch merchant ship would have been a normal sight in the Bahamas.

looking young sailor. He was muscular, handsome, and had beautiful blue eyes. They were often seen walking with their arms linked on the ship's deck. This, of course, angered Calico Jack, who threatened to kill the new sailor if he continued to spend so much time with Anne. Anne confronted the new sailor in a private meeting and told him she was in love with him. She took a big risk by telling this new sailor her feelings for him.

To her disappointment, the handsome sailor told Anne he could not be with her. In fact, he claimed, he was not who he pretended to be. In disbelief, Anne asked what he meant.

The handsome sailor paused, and then revealed this:

"He" was actually a woman. "His" real name was Mary Read.

As they talked more, they became even closer friends. Once Anne told Calico Jack about Mary's identity, he was also very relieved. Mary was a woman, like Anne, who had left her life behind to become a pirate. Anne would have never guessed that Mary Read would prove to be a fierce pirate whose life mirrored Anne's in many ways.

Mary Read was an infamous pirate who grew up dressing as a boy to provide an income for herself and her mother.

Chapter Three
MARY READ

The beginning of Mary Read's life was very similar to Anne Bonny's. Mary was born in London, England around 1690. Mary's father died at sea before Mary was born. Her mother was very worried about how to earn money to support Mary. Unfortunately, Mary's brother had also recently died. Her mother decided to dress Mary in boy's clothes and try to convince her husband's family to still support her and her "son." Mary's grandmother didn't like girls and only boys could inherit money during that time period. If the family found out Mary was a girl, they would stop giving them money.

The scheme worked for a while, and Mary's grandmother sent them money for living expenses. She gave them one crown (a unit of English money) each week, worth about 25¢ then, or around $50 in today's dollars. Mary and her mother would sometimes visit the grandmother with Mary dressed as a boy. During one of these visits, the grandmother grew suspicious that her "grandson" was actually a girl and she stopped sending the pair money. This incident was the first one that showed Mary that, in that time, more value was placed on

DID YOU KNOW?

Mary probably never attended school because in 17th century England, only middle or upper class girls received an education.

boys than on girls. Mary's mother had to find other ways to support herself and her daughter. Since her mother continued to dress Mary in boy's clothes, Mary was able to work as a servant boy and make more money than she would have as a girl.

However, there are other versions of Mary's early life that may also be true. One explains that while her husband was at sea, Mary's mother had a relationship with another man and Mary was born. Around the same time, her son also died. When her husband returned several years later, instead of telling him that his son had died, Mary was dressed in boy's clothes in order to disguise her true identity from her stepfather. A third version of Mary's childhood states that Mary's mother was a widow, and she wished that Mary could have all the benefits of being raised as a boy in a society that provided more opportunities and privileges to boys. Regardless of which version is true, it is an undisputed fact that Mary spent her childhood dressing and acting like a boy.

One of Mary's first jobs as a thirteen year old was as a

In the 1700s in England, servant boys worked for families and ran errands, cleaned, and did odd jobs around the house.

footboy, or a young male servant who ran errands, to a wealthy French woman who lived in a rich neighborhood in London. Over time, Mary found the work boring and imagined a better, more exciting life for herself. The life her father led aboard a ship inspired Mary. She joined the crew aboard a man-of-war ship, a navy vessel, where she worked as a "powder monkey." Powder monkeys were responsible for getting the gunpowder to the men who operated the guns and cannons on a ship. This was the first job a young boy would have had while sailing, and since Mary had been living her entire life as a boy, she was able to work aboard the ship with no one ever suspecting the truth.

Powder monkeys worked very hard on ships to operate the guns and cannons.

While Mary was getting paid more than she would as a servant, the work was

DID YOU KNOW?

Boys as young as nine years old worked as powder monkeys. Some powder monkeys were boys who had been kidnapped and forced to work this dangerous job.

The War of the Spanish Succession (1701–1714) began when Charles II of Spain died. He had no children to take his place. Several European countries, including England, fought for the chance to choose who should become the new king.

often difficult and dangerous and not as exciting as Mary had dreamed it would be. Luckily, she was not injured during her time at sea like many powder monkeys and other young sailors often were. She worked aboard the ship for about three years and then made the decision to join the military. Deployed to Flanders, the northern part of Belgium, she started off in the military as an infantry member. Then, because she was an excellent soldier, she became a member of the cavalry and fought on horseback. She served in the War of the Spanish Succession, which took place from 1701 to 1714, and she proved herself to be a valued member of the military.

While serving in Flanders in the Horse Regiment, she fell in love with a fellow soldier. Up until that point, Mary had hidden her true identity from everyone else. Now, she took a risk and told this soldier that not only was she in love with him, but she was also a woman. She told some members of her regiment that she was a woman and started dressing like a woman for the first time in her life. They accepted her because they had seen that she was a tough soldier. Once she and her husband were married, they both left the army and moved to Breda, in the southern part of the Netherlands. She insisted that she be treated as a proper lady, a lifestyle that Mary had never actually lived. The couple opened an inn and tavern called the Three Horseshoes, and they lived there happily for a brief time. Unfortunately, her husband died of a fever, leaving

Mary a widow after being married only a short while.

Aware of the benefits of being a man during the early 1700s, Mary once again resumed dressing and acting like one. Women in the early 1700s in Europe couldn't vote or own property, and they rarely worked outside of the home or received an education. Mary didn't want to live this type of life, so she rejoined the military, this time in the Netherlands. For a while, she was satisfied with her new life. However, she eventually realized she enjoyed the military less than she had before, perhaps because it brought up memories of her deceased husband. She returned to the only other job she had ever known before—sailing.

Mary joined a Dutch merchant ship that was sailing for the West Indies, otherwise known as the Caribbean. The first interaction Mary had with pirates was when English pirates overtook their ship in the Caribbean. Rather than risk being killed or thrown overboard, Mary joined the pirates. Her experience as a soldier

The West Indies describes a chain of islands more than 2,000 miles long. It consists of islands from Florida to the north coast of Venezuela in South America.

and a sailor provided her with the skills needed to be a fierce pirate who raided ships, fought in duels, and searched for treasure.

Mary's life as a pirate almost came to an end when King George I of England issued a pardon for all pirates who surrendered before September 5, 1718. Piracy was becoming very expensive for European countries who risked losing men, goods, and ships to the pirates, so they were eager to find a solution to this huge problem. The King's Pardon, as it was called, said that any pirate who had killed or stolen while committing piracy would not be charged for those crimes and could return to a regular life without punishment. The treasures the pirates had stolen would remain theirs, unless the people they had stolen from found them and could prove the items were theirs. Another part of the King's Pardon was to pay large amounts of money

King George I was born in Germany in 1660. He was the King of Great Britain for over 12 years, from 1714-1727.

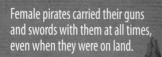
Female pirates carried their guns and swords with them at all times, even when they were on land.

to former pirates to capture pirates who had not surrendered. Pirates who refused to stop their dangerous ways were found and hanged.

Mary, along with many other pirates, signed the pardon in New Providence Island, Bahamas. She joined a privateer—a ship with the sole purpose of finding pirates who had not accepted the pardon—and hunted down pirates still operating in the Caribbean. This was the best way to earn money at the time, live aboard a ship, and not risk punishment. This new arrangement, however, did not last long. Anne Bonny, Calico Jack Rackham, and his crew took over Mary's privateer ship. Instead of honoring their promise to leave piracy behind, Mary and the other former pirates on the ship also joined the crew.

Once Anne Bonny realized Mary—the "man" she had fallen in love with— was actually Mary Read, the two formed a close friendship and often fought side by side. At that time, having even one woman aboard a ship was considered bad luck. Luckily, Calico Jack accepted having two female pirates as a part of his team—he knew first-hand that they were tough.

Yet these were dangerous times for pirates. If a pirate did not take the King's Pardon, he—or she—was at great risk of getting turned in by a former pirate or by government officials. Only time would tell what would happen to Mary Read and Anne Bonny—if they would be able to continue their swashbuckling ways, or if they would get caught . . . and suffer a worse fate.

Mary Read proved herself as a fighter when she won a duel against another pirate. It was only then she felt safe revealing her identity to her fellow pirates.

Chapter Four
ANNE BONNY AND MARY READ

When Anne Bonny and Mary Read met in 1720, they found in each other a rare match—both were female pirates in a male world, both had considerable skills with weapons, both swore and cursed like pirates, and both had left comfortable pasts behind in search of adventure on the high seas. They were accepted by the other men because they had consistently proven themselves as fighters. One incident in particular, which took place soon after she joined Calico Jack's crew, led to Mary's acceptance into the fold.

Mary fell in love with a man named Tom Deane, who had been forced to join the pirates when Calico Jack's crew had taken over his ship. Unfortunately, Tom also caught the attention of a particularly ruthless pirate who challenged Tom to a duel. Tom was not a good fighter. Mary was worried he would be killed, so she challenged the same pirate to a duel before he could hurt Tom, and killed him. Her wild nature and violent temper saved Tom's life. After the fight, she revealed herself as a woman to the rest of the crew because she knew her skill as a fighter could not be denied.

Anne and Mary made a terrifying team and were reported to scream as they boarded and pillaged other ships, showing their weapons, and using them when

DID YOU KNOW?

It is not known how many female pirates there were since they often had to hide their identities. But, many women worked on the sea as servants, launderers, cooks, and sometimes even as merchants, sailors, or naval officers.

necessary. They felt comfortable wearing women's clothes when the ship was at sea. At this point, it had been two years since the King's Pardon. The Royal Governor of the Bahamas, Woodes Rogers, was trying to clean up the Bahamas and make it a safer place to live. Navy ships were sent to find pirates, whose numbers grew fewer and fewer as many of them surrendered. Pirate ships were no longer allowed into ports that had once welcomed them.

The summer and fall of 1720 brought many adventures to Calico Jack and his crew as they sailed near Jamaica, robbing any ship they could find. Often, Anne and Mary would lead the group of pirates who boarded the other boats to steal their trunks of fabrics, bags of gold and silver, and any other valuables they could find.

On October 22, 1720, their streak of luck came to an end. Their boat was anchored close to Point Negril, Jamaica, and they were celebrating their recent good fortune in finding and plundering a merchant ship. The governor of Jamaica had been alerted to the presence of Calico Jack's ship close to shore. He was angry that Calico Jack had not signed the pardon and was trying to rid the Caribbean of pirates. He sent naval captain Jonathan Barnet to hunt them down,

Sailing the waters around Port Negril, Jamaica, was the last time Anne Bonny, Mary Read, and Calico Jack would be pirates together.

Anne Bonny and Mary Read tried their hardest to fight off the British Navy. They were forced to surrender when their crewmates abandoned ship rather than help them.

promising a handsome reward if Calico Jack was captured.

Many of the crew were drunk or below deck drinking and never saw Barnet's boat quietly sneak up beside their own. Anne and Mary were on deck and saw the boat, recognizing that it was a British Navy boat belonging to a pirate hunter working for the governor of Jamaica. They yelled and screamed for their crewmates to join them in fighting. However, some of the crew jumped overboard rather than fight Barnet, who shot off one cannon to warn Calico Jack they were about to take over his ship. Calico Jack started shooting his gun at the governor's ship, but seeing that his men—and women—were unprepared, he surrendered to Barnet.

Anne and Mary were furious that Calico Jack would surrender the *Curlew*, so they started fighting on their own, defending their ship. When Anne realized that the crew was hiding below deck, she yelled for them to join them. It didn't work, so Mary fired her gun into the compartment, killing one of her fellow crewmembers and wounding several others. Barnet's men jumped aboard with their swords and pistols in hand. Anne and Mary had been abandoned by the rest of the crew, yet they put up a good fight, wounding several of the governor's men in the process. They could not believe that their fellow crew members would give up so easily.

Since the two had been celebrating and not planning to fight, they were dressed as women. Barnet's men were unprepared to fight women, especially those who were very good with weapons. When Anne looked up and saw the Jolly Roger on the *Curlew* being replaced by the Union Jack flag, she knew the battle was done. This was the ultimate signal that her life as a pirate was over. They were taken prisoner, along with Calico Jack and the remaining crew members who hadn't abandoned ship or died in the struggle.

All the pirates aboard the *Curlew* faced trial for their crimes in Jamaica. The trial of the crew was popular because word had spread that two of the pirates were female, which most people had never heard of before. Since women at the time were expected to be gentle, loving, and act like proper ladies, this trial caught the imagination of everyone in the audience at the courthouse. If any of the pirates aboard the *Curlew* were able to prove they had been forced to be pirates, they would be freed. Tom was one of these men and avoided being charged with piracy because he had been a crew member of a ship that Calico Jack had conquered.

Captain Calico Jack and eighteen other male pirates were tried on November 16, 1720, in Spanish Town, Jamaica. They were sentenced to death, which was the common punishment for pirates during that time. Anne was able to see Calico Jack before he was killed. She famously told him: "Had you fought like a man, you need not have been hang'd like a dog." She felt he had betrayed her

The British navy led many successful missions to capture pirate ships in the Caribbean.

Many pirates, like Calico Jack, who were found guilty of piracy faced a public hanging.

by not fighting to keep his ship. Calico Jack died on November 18, 1720. The governor made an example of him by proclaiming that any other pirates found would suffer the same death as Calico Jack.

Anne and Mary went to trial for their piracy on November 25, 1720. Former crew members who had been forced to be pirates told the court that the two women were vicious fighters and had acted of their own free will. There was no doubt these women had chosen to be pirates. No one had forced them to fight or steal. The stories these men told the court terrified the jury and audience in the courtroom. One witness, a woman named Dorothy Thomas who had been taken prisoner by Calico Jack's crew for a time, told the court how Anne and Mary threatened her and the other prisoners. Pirate trials were often full of horror and violence, but to hear these same stories, and to know that women had committed them, shocked many of the people in the courtroom. Several American newspapers published articles about the trials. Calico Jack was the subject of most of the stories, along with his two women crew members, but they never mentioned Anne or Mary by name.

Anne and Mary were found guilty. They were also sentenced to death. However, they had both kept a secret from the court until the very moment they were declared guilty. Both Anne and Mary were pregnant. The court was shocked; it had never before had to deal with a pirate who was pregnant, not to mention two pirates who were pregnant! Anne and Mary were put in prison until their babies were born. These prisons were in even worse condition than a ship, and many prisoners died of disease or by starving to death.

Mary was one of those prisoners. She died in prison in 1721 of a fever, along with her unborn baby. She was 31 years old at the time of her death. There is no record of Anne ever being hanged, or of how she left the prison. It is not known for sure where Anne went or if her baby survived. There is doubt as to whether Anne or Mary were actually pregnant—they could have said they were pregnant in order to avoid a death sentence. Anne would have been around 20 years old at the time of her trial. Several stories exist as to what happened to Anne. One suggests her father William became aware of the trial and paid for Anne and her baby to be released to a small island in the Caribbean where she lived for the rest of her life. Another says she moved to England and worked in a tavern, sharing the exciting tales of her

Mary Read died in prison while pregnant.

Prisons during the 18th century were overcrowded because of the horrible living conditions and deadly due to the diseases spread between prisoners.

Pirate legends will always be popular because they are full of danger and adventure.

piracy with her customers.

Women like Anne Bonny and Mary Read were rare in the 1700s. While they certainly had fascinating lives, and the two shared a strong friendship, their lives were full of controversy— they had unpredictable personalities, dressed like men, became murderers, and learned to be skilled fighters and pirates. Mary tragically died in prison, but what happened to Anne? And why was

The mystery surrounding Anne's disappearance has never been solved.

the mystery surrounding her disappearance never solved? Regardless of the fact that we do not know how Anne's story ended, it is true that these two women existed, and that they fulfilled their thirsts for adventure in ways that most women who lived during the 18th century could only read about in newspapers or books. More villains than heroes, Anne Bonny and Mary Read were legendary pirates, and the stories about them are as colorful as the women themselves.

GLOSSARY

controversial: something that creates public debate or disagreement

infatuated: to fall in love with or have strong feelings for

inherit: to receive money or property after someone's death

man-of-war: a nickname for a large British warship armed with cannons

masts: tall upright poles on a ship's deck that support the sails

naval: anything relating to the navy, the part of a country's military forces that fights at sea

New World: a name used by European explorers for the Americas, beginning in the 16th century

pillaged: to steal or rob violently, usually during wartime

plantation: a large property where one specific crop is grown and harvested for commercial sale

port: a place along the coastline where ships can unload and load cargo, usually within a harbor

typhoid: a disease that causes high fevers and stomach pain

BIBLIOGRAPHY

Abbott, Karen. "If There's a Man Among Ye: The Tale of Pirate Queens Anne Bonny and Mary Read." Smithsonian. 9 Aug. 2011. Web. 8 Jan. 2015.

Farquhar, Michael. A Treasury of Foolishly Forgotten Americans: Pirates, Skinflints, Patriots, and Other Colorful Characters Stuck in the Footnotes of History. New York, NY: Penguin, 2008.

Jones, Deanna. "Life in a Man's World: Mary Read." Life in a Man's World: Mary Read. Web. 30 Dec. 2014. www.piratesinfo.com/cpi_Life_in_a_Man's_World:_Mary_Read_531.asp.

McWilliams, K. J. Pirates. New York: F. Watts, 1989.

Pennell, C. R. Bandits at Sea: A Pirates Reader. New York: New York UP, 2001

Roberts, Nancy. Blackbeard and Other Pirates of the Atlantic Coast. Winston-Salem, NC: J.F. Blair, 1993.

Sharp, Anne Wallace. Daring Pirate Women. Minneapolis, MN: Lerner Publications, 2002. "The Legend Of Anne Bonney and Mary Read." The Legend Of Anne Bonney and Mary Read.

Web. 2 Jan. 2015. www.bonney-readkrewe.com/legend.html